Garfield sits around the house

BY: JIM DAVIS

BALLANTINE BOOKS · NEW YORK

All rights reserved under International and Pan-American Copyright
Conventions. Published in the United States by Ballantine Books, a
division of Random House, Inc., New York, and simultaneously in
Canada by Random House of Canada Limited, Toronto, Canada

Library of Congress Catalog Card Number: 83-90066
ISBN: 0-345-31226-0

Manufactured in the United States of America

First Edition: October 1983

10 9 8 7 6 5 4 3 2 1

A GARFIELD NIGHT...

MIDNIGHT SNACK

BREAKFAST

© 1982 United Feature Syndicate, Inc.

© 1982 United Feature Syndicate, Inc.

HOW ARE YOU BOYS GOING TO GET OUT OF THE TREE?

I DON'T KNOW HOW **I'M** GETTING OUT OF THE TREE

© 1982 United Feature Syndicate, Inc. 1-20

AS FOR ODIE...

JIM DAVIS

HEY, GARFIELD, HOW ARE YOU GOING TO GET OUT OF THAT TREE?

1-21

JIM DAVIS

BOING!

BOING!

WHY, BY USING MY HEAD... AND JON'S, AND ODIE'S

© 1982 United Feature Syndicate, Inc.

© 1982 United Feature Syndicate, Inc.

YOU'RE LOOKING A LITTLE STIFF, GARFIELD

1-29

WHAT YOU NEED IS A LEMON TEA RUB AND A GLASS OF HOT HORSE LINIMENT

OR IS THAT A LINIMENT RUB AND A GLASS OF HOT LEMON TEA?

© 1982 United Feature Syndicate, Inc.

GRANDMA'S LEAVING NOW, GARFIELD

JIM DAVIS   1-30

SO LONG, GRANDMA

SO LONG, GARFIELD

YOU LIKED HER DIDN'T YOU, GARFIELD?

BACK WHEN THEY MADE HER, THINGS WERE BUILT TO LAST

© 1982 United Feature Syndicate, Inc.

RRRR

GARFIELD! LUNCH TIME!

JIM DAVIS   1-31

GARFIELD! WHERE ARE YOU?

SCREEE

IT IS TIME FOR YOU TO EAT, YOUR MAJESTY

IF I MUST

GARFIELD

© 1982 United Feature Syndicate, Inc.

KABOOM

I HATE MONDAY

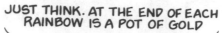

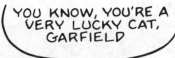

WE MUST DO SOMETHING ABOUT YOUR BREATH, GARFIELD

IT'S NOT MY FAULT YOU LEFT THE GARLIC CHEESE OUT LAST NIGHT

RATHER THAN FIX YOUR BREAKFAST EVERY DAY, GARFIELD, I'VE DECIDED TO LET YOU SERVE YOURSELF

MAYBE THAT WASN'T SUCH A GOOD IDEA

I DON'T BELIEVE I ATE THAT WHOLE BAG OF CAT FOOD

JIM DAVIS 2-17

I'D BETTER JOG SOME OF THIS TUMMY OFF

I REALLY DON'T LIKE MYSELF WHEN I'M THIS FAT

JIM DAVIS 2-18

SWIPE!

I CAN'T EVEN ENJOY THE SIMPLE PLEASURES IN LIFE

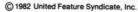

I HATE MONDAYS

© 1982 United Feature Syndicate, Inc.   2-22

JIM DAVIS   2-23

© 1982 United Feature Syndicate, Inc.

JUST STAYING IN SHAPE IN CASE I EVER GET THAT HUNGRY

OKAY, GARFIELD. ONE BITE

COUGH COUGH

GASP!

OKAY, NO MORE DRY CAT FOOD

PHOBIAS ARE FUNNY THINGS

I AM ABSOLUTELY FEARLESS EXCEPT WHERE SPIDERS ARE CONCERNED

HELLO, SNAKE

HOW ARE YOU?

ISN'T THAT STRANGE? SPIDERS SCARE ME, BUT SNAKES DON'T SCARE ME

2-28   JIM DAVIS

NOW SNAKES SCARE ME

© 1982 United Feature Syndicate, Inc.

SMACK!
SLURP!

YOU HAVE THE MANNERS
OF A PIG, GARFIELD.
SLOW DOWN AND
SPIT OUT THE SEEDS

JIM DAVIS 3-5

RATA TATA
TATA TATA

© 1982 United Feature Syndicate, Inc.

JIM DAVIS 3-6

© 1982 United Feature Syndicate, Inc.

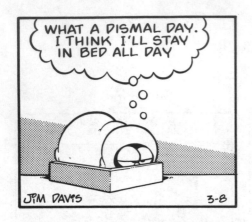

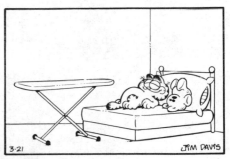

© 1982 United Feature Syndicate, Inc.   3-21   JIM DAVIS

ROWR

© 1982 United Feature Syndicate, Inc.

JIM DAVIS

3-22

BOOT

AND NOW FOR THE MAIN ATTRACTION

TESTING, ONE, TWO. TESTING, ONE, TWO

ROWR

3-23

© 1982 United Feature Syndicate, Inc.

CAN YOU HEAR ME THERE IN THE BACK?

GOOD

JIM DAVIS

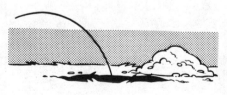

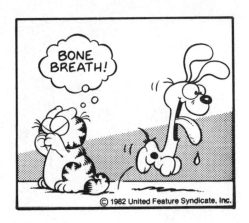

© 1982 United Feature Syndicate, Inc.

JIM DAVIS

4-4

FOOM!

BOINK

BEEP! BEEP!

BZT

© 1982 United Feature Syndicate, Inc.

JUST AS I THOUGHT, ALL THE WARRANTIES EXPIRED YESTERDAY

JIM DAVIS

4-11

FOOD, FOOD, FOOD, IS THAT ALL YOU THINK ABOUT, GARFIELD?

THAT'S ABOUT IT

4-14

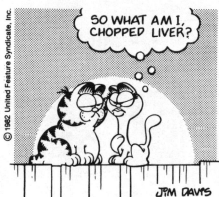

SO WHAT AM I, CHOPPED LIVER?

JIM DAVIS

DON'T FLATTER YOURSELF

HE CERTAINLY KNOWS HOW TO MAKE A GIRL FEEL GOOD

DO YOU KNOW WHAT I LIKE ABOUT WOMEN?

JIM DAVIS

4-15

THEY ARE SO SOFT

COME TO THINK OF IT...

I LOVE TELEVISION

WHERE ELSE CAN YOU SEE SIGNIFICANT WORLD EVENTS? WHERE ELSE CAN YOU SEE THE GREAT OPERA AND BALLET?

WHERE ELSE CAN YOU SEE LORENZO THE WOODCHUCK RACE A STEAM LOCOMOTIVE OVER RICKY THE RAT?

4-26

© 1982 United Feature Syndicate, Inc.

WHY ALL THIS FLAP ABOUT TELEVISION?

THEY SAY FAMILIES DON'T VISIT ANYMORE...

WHY, THAT'S WHAT COMMERCIALS ARE FOR

4-27

© 1982 United Feature Syndicate, Inc.

JIM DAVIS

I GOTTA FIX THAT VERTICAL HOLD

WE'LL BE RIGHT BACK AFTER THIS WORD FROM OUR SPONSOR

"SASQUATCH"

WELCOME BACK

HURRY UP WITH THAT HAY, SON. SUPPER'S WAITIN'

5-7 JIM DAVIS

SON?

LONG TIME, NO FARM, HUH, JON?

WE HAD FUN VISITING THE FARM, DIDN'T WE, GARFIELD?

SPEAK FOR YOURSELF, JON

JIM DAVIS 5-8

IT'S GREAT GETTING BACK TO BASICS, PUTTING YOUR HANDS IN OLD MOTHER EARTH

BUT I'LL NEVER GET THESE FINGERNAILS CLEAN

A REAL MAN OF THE LAND

JUST WHAT IS TELEVISION?

TELEVISION NOT ONLY GIVES THE EYEBALLS SOMETHING TO DO,

© 1982 United Feature Syndicate, Inc.

BUT IT'S A SOCIALLY ACCEPTABLE EXCUSE TO SNACK

5-12

JIM DAVIS

JUST WHAT IS A GOLDFISH?

JIM DAVIS

5-13

A GOLDFISH IS AN AQUATIC EXPRESSION OF BEAUTY AND GRACE THAT PROVIDES ITS OBSERVERS WITH MANY HOURS OF BLISSFUL MEDITATION

© 1982 United Feature Syndicate, Inc.

IT ALSO MAKES A DARN FINE BREAKFAST

JUST WHAT IS A DOG?

JIM DAVIS 5-14

LET ME PUT IT THIS WAY...

IF A DOG WERE A FAUCET, IT WOULD LEAK

© 1982 United Feature Syndicate, Inc.

JUST WHAT IS A CAT? A CAT IS A FURRY ANIMAL, COMPLETE WITH DOG NIBBLERS AND FURNITURE SHREDDERS

JIM DAVIS 5-15

HACK!

THE HAIRBALLS IN THE THROAT ARE ALSO STANDARD EQUIPMENT

© 1982 United Feature Syndicate, Inc.

YAWN

WHAT HAPPENED TO YOU?

I GOT UP ON THE WRONG SIDE OF THE BED

JIM DAVIS 5-17

JIM DAVIS 5-18

CHUG!

YOU'RE A REAL BEAR UNTIL YOU'VE HAD YOUR FIRST CUP OF COFFEE, AREN'T YOU?

AND THEN I'M THE SWEETEST SO-AND-SO AROUND

© 1982 United Feature Syndicate, Inc.

JIM DAVIS

JIM DAVIS
5-31

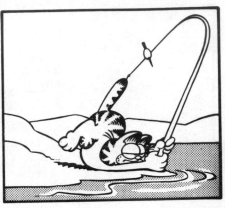

6-1

JIM DAVIS

WAH-CHOO!

WAH-CHOO!

I LOVE YOU, BUNNY RABBIT

I LOVE YOU, TOO, DEER

I LOVE YOU ALL

WHAT THE...?

I BROUGHT SOME FRIENDS HOME FOR DINNER

JIM DAVIS 9-6

© 198_ United Feature Syndicate, Inc.

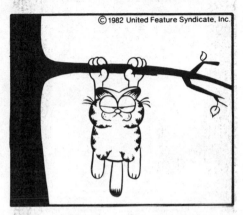

YAWN

6-16

YOU KNOW YOU'RE GETTING OLDER WHEN YOUR FAVORITE LATE NIGHT SHOW IS THE SIX O'CLOCK NEWS

6-17

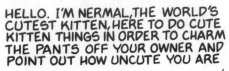
HELLO. I'M NERMAL, THE WORLD'S CUTEST KITTEN, HERE TO DO CUTE KITTEN THINGS IN ORDER TO CHARM THE PANTS OFF YOUR OWNER AND POINT OUT HOW UNCUTE YOU ARE

I HATE MONDAY

© 1982 United Feature Syndicate, Inc.

GIMME THAT

I FAIL TO SEE WHAT'S SO CUTE ABOUT YARN

OR KITTENS, FOR THAT MATTER

© 1982 United Feature Syndicate, Inc.

GEE, SINCE NERMAL ISN'T HERE, I'LL EAT HIS FOOD, TOO

© 1982 United Feature Syndicate, Inc.

OKAY, NERMAL, GO AHEAD AND JUMP

I'LL HAVE YOU OUT OF THERE IN TWO SHAKES OF A CAT'S TAIL

© 1982 United Feature Syndicate, Inc.

OR IS THAT, TWO SHAKES OF A LAMB'S TAIL?

SPLAT!

6-28

IT'S TIME YOU GO ON ANOTHER DIET, GARFIELD

JUST WHAT IS A DIET?

6-29

A DIET IS TOO LITTLE OF A GOOD THING. A DIET IS MAKING A MOLEHILL OUT OF A MOUNTAIN

A DIET IS THE SUBJECT OF A LOT OF STUPID PLATITUDES

THAT APPLE IS ALL YOU'RE GETTING FOR DINNER, GARFIELD

JIM DAVIS   7-2

© 1982 United Feature Syndicate, Inc.

GIMME FOOD. LOTS OF IT. AND RIGHT NOW

JIM DAVIS   7-3

YES, SIR

© 1982 United Feature Syndicate, Inc.

TWO ADJECTIVES NEVER USED TO DESCRIBE A CAT ARE: "WISHY" AND "WASHY"

THERE MUST BE MORE TO LIFE THAN THIS. I'M GOING TO FIND SOME EXCITEMENT

YUK!

YOU'RE OUT OF YOUR TERRITORY, AREN'T YOU, FELLA?

© 1982 United Feature Syndicate, Inc.

HELLO THERE, STRAY CAT

POUND

WHERE HAVE YOU BEEN?

CULTIVATING A HEALTHY DISLIKE FOR EXCITEMENT

JIM DAVIS

7-4

IN OUR FAST-PACED WORLD, RELAXATION IS PRACTICALLY A LOST ART

7-5

JIM DAVIS

Z

PRACTICALLY

© 1982 United Feature Syndicate, Inc.

HERE YOU GO, GARFIELD

TABLE SCRAPS!

GARFIELD

JIM DAVIS

7-6

SPLAT!

GARFIELD

THAT'S DOG FOOD

GARFIELD

© 1982 United Feature Syndicate, Inc.

7-9

DON'T LOOK IN HERE, JON. IT'S NOT A PRETTY SIGHT

I WISH JON WOULD GET MARRIED

JIM DAVIS

7-10

FWEEE

THE ONLY WAY HE KNOWS MY DINNER IS READY, IS WHEN IT SETS OFF THE SMOKE ALARM

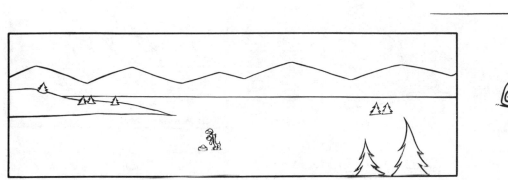

TOUCH MY FOOD AND YOU'RE ONE DEAD DOG

© 1982 United Feature Syndicate, Inc.

JIM DAVIS

7-11

GOBBLE! SMACK! SLURP!

JIM DAVIS 7-14

GARFIELD!

UH-OH

STAY RIGHT WHERE YOU ARE OR THE TEDDY BEAR GETS IT

© 1982 United Feature Syndicate, Inc.

YOU LEAD A VERY SPECIAL LIFE, POOKY

JIM DAVIS 7-15

YOU DON'T HAVE TO FIGHT WITH DOGS. YOU DON'T HAVE TO SLEEP. YOU DON'T HAVE TO EAT

I FEEL SORRY FOR YOU

© 1982 United Feature Syndicate, Inc.

JIM DAVIS

7-16

7-17

JIM DAVIS

I KNOW, I KNOW

GARFIELD, I WOULDN'T SAY YOU'RE FAT...

JIM DAVIS

BUT HERMAN MELVILLE WANTS TO WRITE A BOOK ABOUT YOU

7-21

SPLUT

GARFIELD

© 1982 United Feature Syndicate, Inc.

UH-OH! TOO HARD!

JIM DAVIS

WHY HAVEN'T THOSE EGGS COME DOWN? MAYBE THEY STUCK TO THE CEILING. MAYBE I SHOULD LOOK

7-22

SPLUT

© 1982 United Feature Syndicate, Inc.

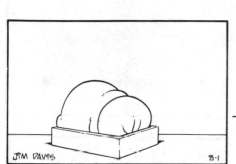

© 1982 United Feature Syndicate, Inc.

3-8 JIM DAVIS

Here is the Paws, Incorporated staff — the faces behind the cat — with their noses to the grindstone, shoulders to the wheel, ears to the ground, and faces to the picture window.

Top row, left to right: Mike Fentz, Artist; Valette Hildebrand, Assistant Cartoonist; Larry Carmichael, Pilot; Ron Tuthill, Production Manager; Dave Kühn, Artist; Dave Davis, Artist; Brian Lum, Artist; and Kevin Campbell, Artist.

Bottom row, left to right: Dick Hamilton, Business Manager; Neil Altekruse, Artist; Linda Sissom, Office Manager; Jill Hahn, Licensing Assistant; Jim Davis, Garfield Creator; Sheila Bolduc, Traffic Manager; and Julie Hamilton, President.